PIANO • VOCAL • GUITAR

S0-BJU-260

TOP CHRISTIAN HITS

2016-2017

ISBN 978-1-4950-9065-3

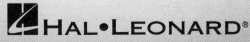

7777 W. BLUEMOUND RD. P.O. BOX 13819 MILWAUKEE, WI 53213

Visit Hal Leonard Online at
www.halleonard.com

CHAIN BREAKER

Words and Music by JONATHAN SMITH,
MIA FIELDES and ZACH WILLIAMS

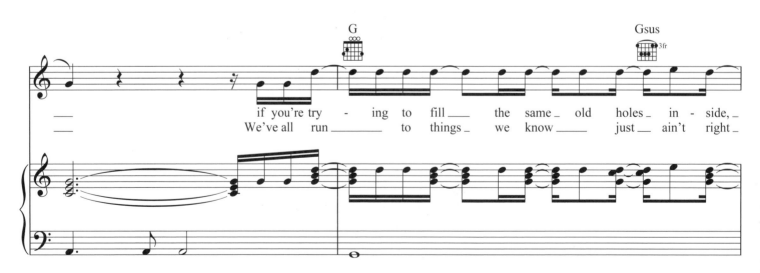

CHRIST IN ME

Words and Music by JEREMY CAMP
and BERNIE HERMS

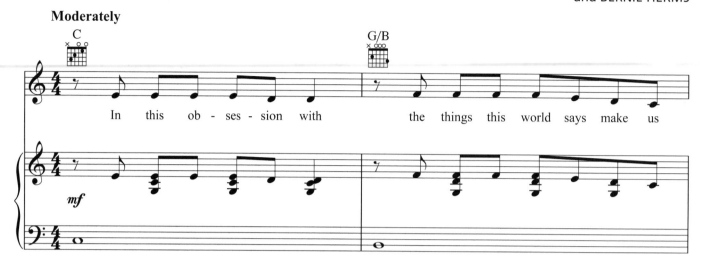

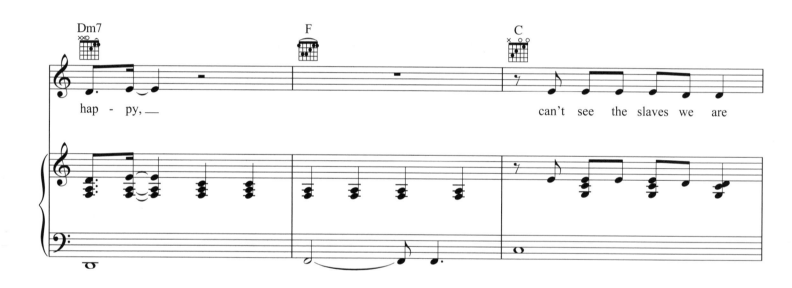

9

DEAR YOUNGER ME

Words and Music by BART MILLARD,
MIKE SCHEUCHZER, NATHAN COCHRAN,
ROBSHAFFER, BARRY GRAUL,
DAVID GARCIA and BEN GLOVER

Cmaj7
G
You are ho - ly, you are right - eous, you are one
Em
Bm
of the re - deemed, set a - part, a brand - new heart; oh,
Repeat and Fade
Cmaj7
you are free in - deed. You are ho -
Optional Ending
Cmaj7
you are free in - deed.
G
rit.

COME ALIVE
(Dry Bones)

Words and Music by LAUREN DAIGLE
and MICHAEL FARREN

Moderate Power Ballad

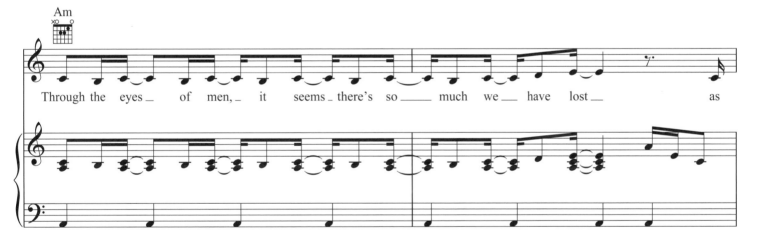

Through the eyes _ of men, _ it seems _ there's so ___ much we _ have lost _ as

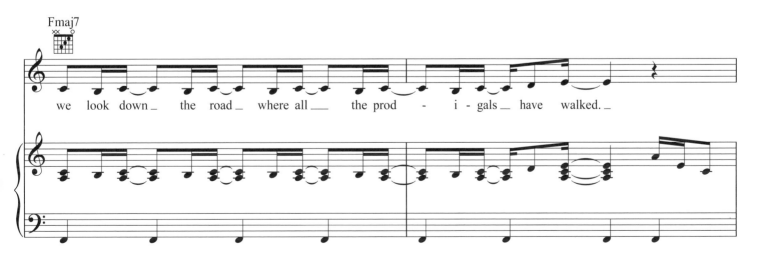

we look down _ the road _ where all ___ the prod - i - gals _ have walked. _

We call out to dead __ hearts, "Come a - live, _____ come a - live." _____

Up out of the ash - es, let __ us see ___ an ar - my rise. __

We call out to dry __ bones, "Come a - live." _____ Yeah, _____

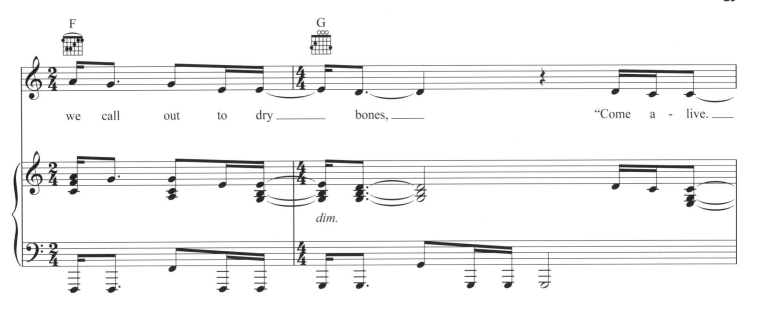

we call out to dry _____ bones, _____ "Come a - live. _____

dim.

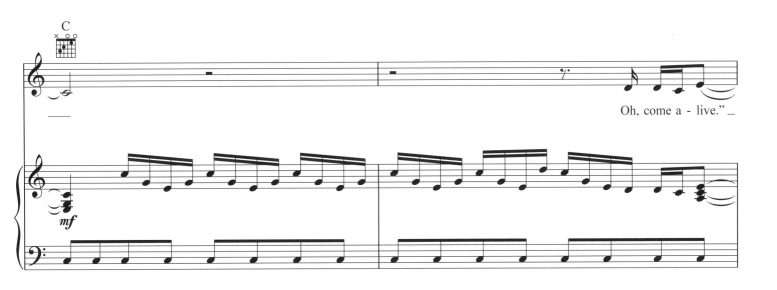

_____ Oh, come a - live." _

mf

EYE OF THE STORM

Words and Music by BRYAN FOWLER
and RYAN STEVENSON

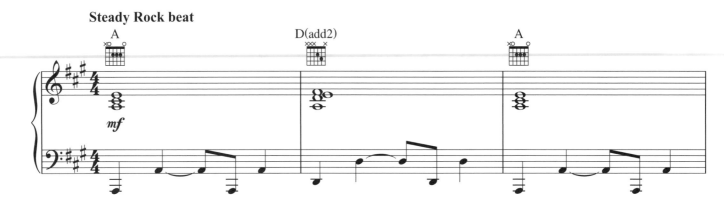

When the sol - id ground _ is fall - ing out _ from
hopes and dreams _ are far from me _ and I'm

un - der - neath _ my feet, _ be - tween the black skies _ and my red _ eyes,
run - ning out _ of faith, _ I see the fu - ture _ I _ pic - ture _

FIERCE

Words and Music by CHRIS QUILALA,
JOSH SILVERBERG and MIA FIELDES

IF WE'RE HONEST

Words and Music by MOLLY REED,
FRANCESCA BATTISTELLI and JEFF PARDO

Moderate Ballad

Truth is hard-er than a lie, the dark seems saf-er than the light, and ev-'ry-one has a heart that loves to hide. _

JESUS

Words and Music by CHRIS TOMLIN
and ED CASH

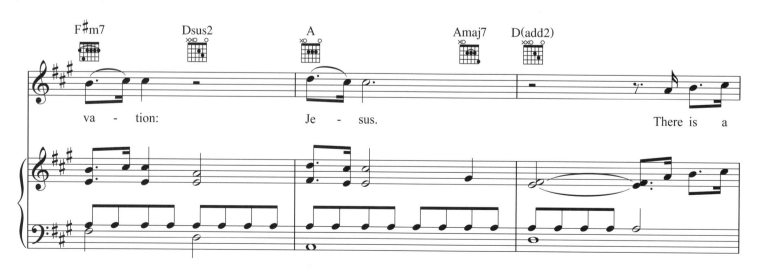

KING OF THE WORLD

Words and Music by SAMUEL MIZELL,
NATALIE GRANT and BECCA MIZELL

* Recorded a half step lower.

THE LION AND THE LAMB

Words and Music by BRENTON BROWN,
BRIAN JOHNSON and LEELAND MOORING

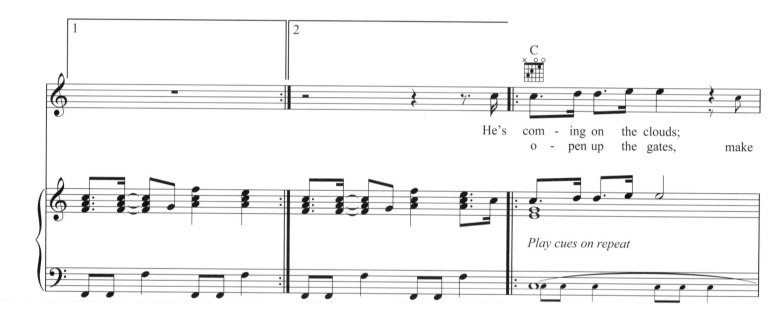

He's com - ing on the clouds;
o - pen up the gates, make

Play cues on repeat

kings and king - doms will bow down.
way be - fore the King of kings.

And
Our

* Recorded a half step lower.

GRACE WINS

Words and Music by
MATTHEW WEST

With energy

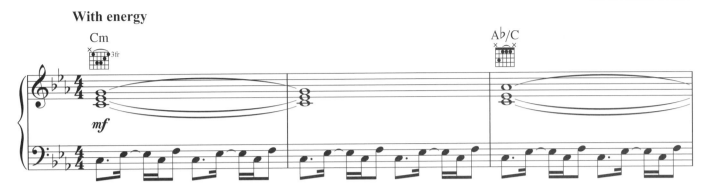

In my weak-est mo-ment, I ___ see

You shak-ing Your _ head in ___ dis-

MY VICTORY

Words and Music by DAVID CROWDER,
DARREN MULLIGAN, ED CASH
and HANK BENTLEY

death is hell's de - feat. A cross meant to kill is my

vic - to - ry. ___ Oh, a cross meant to kill is my vic - to - ry. ___

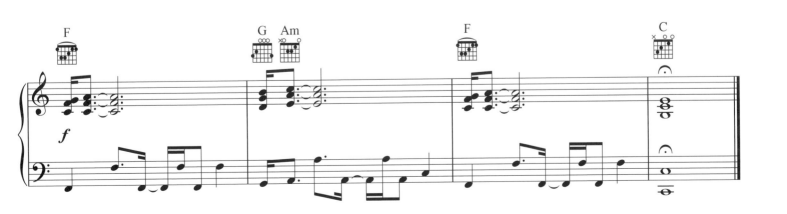

ONE STEP AWAY

Words and Music by MATTHEW WEST,
BERNIE HERMS and JOHN MARK HALL

Moderate Rock beat

What if you could go back and re - live one
far you've gone;

day of your life all o - ver a - gain,_ and un - make the mis - take that
mer - cy says you don't have to keep a - run - nin' down the road you're on.

left you a mil - lion miles a - way_ from the you you once knew? Now
Love's nev - er met a lost cause. Your shame, lay it down. Leave your

Recorded a half step lower.

PRICELESS

Words and Music by JOEL SMALLBONE,
LUKE SMALLBONE, SETH MOSLEY,
TEDD TJORNHOM and BENJAMIN BACKUS

Recorded a half step lower.

RISE

Words and Music by DANNY GOKEY,
JOSH BRONLEEWE and BENJI COWART

SLOW DOWN

Words and Music by CHRIS STEVENS
and NICHOLE NORDEMAN

THY WILL

Words and Music by BERNIE HERMS,
EMILY WEISBAND and HILLARY SCOTT

TESTIFY

Words and Music by NATHANIEL RINEHART
and WILLIAM RINEHART

Acoustic Folk Rock

Give _ me your heart, give _ me your song, sing _ it with all your might. _

Come _ to the foun - tain _ and you _ can be sat - is - fied. _ There _ is a peace, there _ is a

love, you _ can get lost in - side. _ Come _ to the foun - tain _ and

YOU ARE LOVED

Words and Music by JEFF SOJKA,
JOSH ZEGAN, CHRIS CLEVELAND
and KYLE WILLIAMS

Rhythmic Ballad

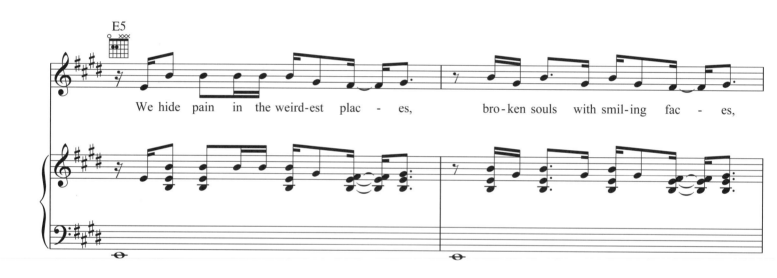

We hide pain in the weird-est plac - es, bro-ken souls with smil-ing fac - es,

fight-ing for __ sur-ren-der for now and __ the af-ter, yeah. __

WHAT A BEAUTIFUL NAME

Words and Music by BEN FIELDING
and BROOKE LIGERTWOOD

124

CONTEMPORARY CHRISTIAN FOLIOS
FROM HAL LEONARD

Arranged for Piano, Voice and Guitar

CASTING CROWNS – THRIVE
Our matching folio features all the tracks from this popular Christian band's 2014 album which has topped the Billboard® Christian Albums Chart, including the lead single "All You've Ever Wanted," plus: Broken Together • Dream for You • Follow Me • House of Their Dreams • Just Be Held • Love You with the Truth • Thrive • You Are the Only One • and more.
00125333 P/V/G..$16.99

CASTING CROWNS – THE VERY NEXT THING
All 12 tracks from the multi-platinum selling Christian group's 2016 album are featured in arrangements for piano, voice and guitar. Includes the singles "One Step Away" and "The Very Next Thing," plus: For All You Are • God of All My Days • Loving My Jesus • Make Me a River • No Other Name • Song That the Angels Can't Sing • What If I Gave Everything • and more.
00196585 P/V/G..$16.99

CHRISTIAN CHART HITS
30 favorites from beloved Christian artists such as Kari Jobe, Jeremy Camp, Third Day, Danny Gokey, and others arranged for piano, voice and guitar. Songs include: All the People Said Amen • Blessings • Day One • Forever (We Sing Hallelujah) • Good to Be Alive • He Knows • I Need a Miracle • Lead Me • Overcomer • Tell Your Heart to Beat Again • Trust in You • We Believe • Write Your Story • You Are More • and more.
00194583 P/V/G..$16.99

THE VERY BEST OF HILLSONG
25 songs from the popular worldwide church including: Came to My Rescue • From the Inside Out • Hosanna • I Give You My Heart • Lead Me to the Cross • Mighty to Save • Shout to the Lord • The Stand • Worthy Is the Lamb • and more.
00312101 P/V/G..$17.99

HILLSONG MODERN WORSHIP HITS
20 songs, including: Alive • Broken Vessels (Amazing Grace) • Christ Is Enough • Cornerstone • Forever Reign • God Is Able • Mighty to Save • Oceans (Where Feet May Fail) • The Stand • This I Believe (The Creed) • Touch the Sky • and more.
00154952 P/V/G..$16.99

THIRD DAY – LEAD US BACK: SONGS OF WORSHIP
All 12 tracks from Third Day's first collection of all-original worship songs: Father of Lights • He Is Alive • I Know You Can • In Jesus Name • Lead Us Back • Maker • The One I Love • Our Deliverer • Soul on Fire • Spirit • Victorious • Your Words.
00145263 P/V/G..$16.99

TIMELESS CHRISTIAN SONGS
24 CCM & Gospel Favorites
A great collection of new and classic standards in Christian music, including: Amazing Grace (My Chains Are Gone) • Because He Lives • Friends • How Great Is Our God • I Can Only Imagine • Lamb of God • 10,000 Reasons (Bless the Lord) • Thy Word • and more.
00137799 P/V/G..$16.99

CHRIS TOMLIN – LOVE RAN RED
Matching piano/vocal/guitar arrangements to Tomlin's 2014 release featuring 12 tracks: Almighty • At the Cross (Love Ran Red) • Fear Not • Greater • Jesus Loves Me • The Roar • Waterfall • and more.
00139166 P/V/G..$16.99

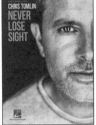

CHRIS TOMLIN – NEVER LOSE SIGHT
"America's Worship Leader" is back with this 2016 release featuring 14 new tracks including the hit singles "Good Good Father" and "Jesus." Other songs include: All Yours • Come Thou Fount (I Will Sing) • First Love • Glory Be • God and God Alone • The God I Know • God of Calvary • He Lives • Home • Impossible Things • Kyrie Eleison • Yes and Amen.
00201955 P/V/G..$16.99

TOP CHRISTIAN HITS 2015-2016
22 top hits, including: At the Cross (Love Ran Red) • Because He Lives, Amen • Brother • Drops in the Ocean • First • Flawless • Holy Spirit • Same Power • Soul on Fire • Through All of It • and more.
00154720 P/V/G..$16.99

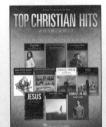

TOP CHRISTIAN HITS 2016-2017
20 favorite releases, including: Chain Breaker • Christ in Me • Dear Younger Me • Eye of the Storm • Grace Wins • If We're Honest • King of the World • The Lion and the Lamb • Priceless • Rise • Thy Will • What a Beautiful Name • You Are Loved • and more.
00225283 P/V/G..$16.99

THE BEST OF MATTHEW WEST
16 top singles from popular Christian artist Matthew West arranged for piano, voice and guitar. Includes: Do Something • Forgiveness • Grace Wins • Hello, My Name Is • Mended • Only Grace • Strong Enough • When I Say I Do • You Are Everything • and more.
00159489 P/V/G..$16.99

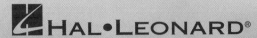

HAL•LEONARD®
For a complete listing of the products we have available, visit us online at **www.halleonard.com**

The Best
PRAISE & WORSHIP
Songbooks for Piano

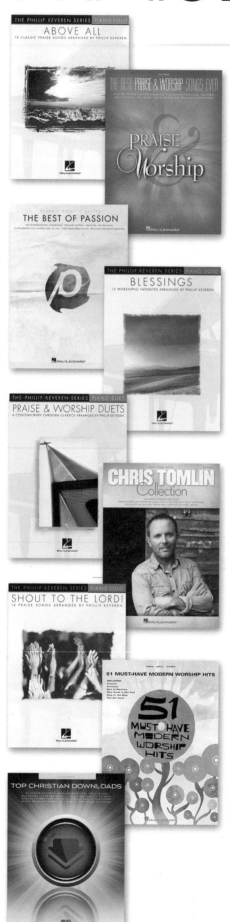

Above All
THE PHILLIP KEVEREN SERIES
15 beautiful praise song piano solo arrangements by Phillip Keveren. Includes: Above All • Agnus Dei • Breathe • Draw Me Close • He Is Exalted • I Stand in Awe • Step by Step • We Fall Down • You Are My King (Amazing Love) • and more.
00311024 Piano Solo..................................$11.95

Blessings
THE PHILLIP KEVEREN SERIES
Phillip Keveren delivers another stellar collection of piano solo arrangements perfect for any reverent or worship setting: Blessed Be Your Name • Blessings • Cornerstone • Holy Spirit • This Is Amazing Grace • We Believe • Your Great Name • Your Name • and more.
00156601 Piano Solo $12.99

The Best Praise & Worship Songs Ever
80 all-time favorites: Awesome God • Breathe • Days of Elijah • Here I Am to Worship • I Could Sing of Your Love Forever • Open the Eyes of My Heart • Shout to the Lord • We Bow Down • dozens more.
00311057 P/V/G $22.99

More of the Best Praise & Worship Songs Ever
76 more contemporary worship favorites, including: Beautiful One • Everlasting God • Friend of God • How Great Is Our God • In Christ Alone • Let It Rise • Mighty to Save • Your Grace Is Enough • more.
00311800 P/V/G $24.99

The Big Book of Praise & Worship
Over 50 worship favorites are presented in this popular "Big Book" series collection. Includes: Always • Cornerstone • Forever Reign • I Will Follow • Jesus Paid It All • Lord, I Need You • Mighty to Save • Our God • Stronger • 10,000 Reasons (Bless the Lord) • This Is Amazing Grace • and more.
00140795 P/V/G $22.99

Contemporary Worship Duets
arr. Bill Wolaver
Contains 8 powerful songs carefully arranged by Bill Wolaver as duets for intermediate-level players: Agnus Dei • Be unto Your Name • He Is Exalted • Here I Am to Worship • I Will Rise • The Potter's Hand • Revelation Song • Your Name.
00290593 Piano Duets $10.99

51 Must-Have Modern Worship Hits
A great collection of 51 of today's most popular worship songs, including: Amazed • Better Is One Day • Everyday • Forever • God of Wonders • He Reigns • How Great Is Our God • Offering • Sing to the King • You Are Good • and more.
00311428 P/V/G $22.99

Hillsong Worship Favorites
12 powerful worship songs arranged for piano solo: At the Cross • Came to My Rescue • Desert Song • Forever Reign • Holy Spirit Rain Down • None but Jesus • The Potter's Hand • The Stand • Stronger • and more.
00312522 Piano Solo..................................$12.99

The Best of Passion
Over 40 worship favorites featuring the talents of David Crowder, Matt Redman, Chris Tomlin, and others. Songs include: Always • Awakening • Blessed Be Your Name • Jesus Paid It All • My Heart Is Yours • Our God • 10,000 Reasons (Bless the Lord) • and more.
00101888 P/V/G $19.99

Praise & Worship Duets
THE PHILLIP KEVEREN SERIES
8 worshipful duets by Phillip Keveren: As the Deer • Awesome God • Give Thanks • Great Is the Lord • Lord, I Lift Your Name on High • Shout to the Lord • There Is a Redeemer • We Fall Down.
00311203 Piano Duet $11.95

Shout to the Lord!
THE PHILLIP KEVEREN SERIES
14 favorite praise songs, including: As the Deer • El Shaddai • Give Thanks • Great Is the Lord • How Beautiful • More Precious Than Silver • Oh Lord, You're Beautiful • A Shield About Me • Shine, Jesus, Shine • Shout to the Lord • Thy Word • and more.
00310699 Piano Solo $12.95

The Chris Tomlin Collection – 2nd Edition
15 songs from one of the leading artists and composers in Contemporary Christian music, including the favorites: Amazing Grace (My Chains Are Gone) • Holy Is the Lord • How Can I Keep from Singing • How Great Is Our God • Jesus Messiah • Our God • We Fall Down • and more.
00306951 P/V/G $16.99

Top Christian Downloads
21 of Christian music's top hits are presented in this collection of intermediate level piano solo arrangements. Includes: Forever Reign • How Great Is Our God • Mighty to Save • Praise You in This Storm • 10,000 Reasons (Bless the Lord) • Your Grace Is Enough • and more.
00125051 Piano Solo..................................$14.99

Top Worship Downloads
20 of today's chart-topping Christian hits, including: Cornerstone • Forever Reign • Great I Am • Here for You • Lord, I Need You • My God • Never Once • One Thing Remains (Your Love Never Fails) • Your Great Name • and more.
00120870 P/V/G $16.99

HAL•LEONARD®
www.halleonard.com
P/V/G = Piano/Vocal/Guitar Arrangements
Prices, contents, and availability subject to change without notice.
0317